HEALING
POWER
OF THE
ROOTS

It's a Matter of *Life* and *Death*

DOMINIQUAE
BIERMAN, PHD

THE HEALING POWER OF THE ROOTS © 1996–2020
by Archbishop Dr. Dominiquae Bierman
Published by Zion's Gospel Press
52 Tuscan Way, Ste 202-412
St. Augustine, FL, 32092
shalom@zionsgospel.com
Printed in the United States of America

Unless otherwise identified, Scripture quotations are from the King James Version or New American Standard Bible.
NASB © Copyright 1960, 1962, 1963, 1968, 1971, 1972, 1973, 1975, 1977 The Lockman Foundation. Used by permission. All rights reserved.

On occasion, words such as Jesus, Christ, LORD, and God have been changed by the author, back to their original Hebrew renderings: Yeshua, Messiah, Yahveh, and ELOHIM.
Bold emphasis or underlining within quotations is the author's own.

Paperback ISBN: 978-1-953502-08-7
E-Book ISBN: 978-1-953502-09-4

First printing: June 2005, Second printing: April 2007, Third printing: May 2011, Fourth printing: July 2018, Fifth printing: August 2020

ZIONS GOSPEL
PRESS

This book is dedicated to all of God's children,
wherever they may be.

Early Messianic Symbol

This sign has been found on pottery and walls of what is believed to be the meeting rooms in Jerusalem of second-century believers in Yeshua. During archaeological excavations in recent years, this symbol (with variations) has been found repeatedly.

Experts now feel that it was a sign of unity between the Jewish believers and their Christian brethren in the rest of the Roman Empire. It has been suggested that it was also a secret symbol of identification in times of persecution.

Acknowledgments

First, I would like to give thanks to the God of Israel who did not spare His own Son so that I might be reconciled with Him and with my roots as a Jew. He alone has made me whole and has given me the ability to write and the power to love.

I also want to thank my beloved husband, Baruch. His encouragement and enthusiasm and practical help have been a constant source of strength.

Finally, I would like to thank Max and Erika Stickel from Switzerland, who compelled me to stay and write while they took care of my every need.

Thank you for eternity!—Archbishop Dr. Dominiquae Bierman

Dear Reader

I hope that the LORD will speak to you through this book. I am fully aware that there is a lot more to say about this important subject. I do not presume to have the last word about it. I do not even presume that I am a hundred percent theologically correct. I believe that is reserved for the Holy Spirit alone, as He is our teacher. My purpose in writing this book is to be a vessel of God's truth and healing, as we all watch the most amazing restoration of all times happen before our very eyes, that is, the restoration of Israel. As you read, you will know that you are "grafted into" Israel and that you are a very important part of this restoration. A new reformation is knocking at the doors of the church. Some will tend to resist it. My prayer is that this book will be a tool in God's hands to facilitate our yielding to this new move of restoration, back to our roots.

For His glory, your friend and His Archbishop,
—Dr. Dominiquae Bierman

Contents

It is the glory of God to conceal a matter,
but the glory of kings is to search out a matter.

PROVERBS 25:2

But you are a chosen race, a royal priesthood, a holy nation, a
people for God's own possession, so that you may proclaim the
excellencies of Him who has called you out of darkness
into His marvelous light;

1 PETER 2:9

For I do not want you, brethren, to be uninformed of this
mystery—so that you will not be wise in your own estimation—
that a partial hardening has happened to Israel until the fullness
of the Gentiles has come in; and so all Israel will be saved; just as
it is written, "The Deliverer will come from Zion,
He will remove ungodliness from Jacob."

ROMANS 11:25-26

The glory which You have given Me I have given to them, that
they may be one, just as We are one; I in them and You in Me,
that they may be perfected in unity, so that the world may know
that You sent Me, and loved them, even as You have loved Me.

JOHN 17: 22-23

"And you, son of man, take for yourself one stick and write on it,
'For Judah and for the sons of Israel, his companions'; then take
another stick and write on it, 'For Joseph, the stick of Ephraim
and all the house of Israel, his companions.' Then join them for

yourself one to another into one stick,
that they may become one in your hand.

EZEKIEL 37:16-17

My people are destroyed for lack of knowledge. Because you
have rejected knowledge, I also will reject you from being My
priest. Since you have forgotten the law of your God,
I also will forget your children.

HOSEA 4:6

CHAPTER ONE

A Killing Arrogance

"Do not be arrogant toward the branches; but if you are arrogant, remember that it is not you who supports the root, but the root supports you... For if God did not spare the natural branches, neither will He spare you..."

—ROMANS 11:18,21

So, what's the 'big deal' of ministering the 'roots' to the church?" I asked the Holy Spirit of God while onboard the El Al flight from Zurich to Tel Aviv. I wanted to understand the purpose of traveling to so many nations – *"God, what are you saying?"*

Still very vivid in my mind were the testimonies of miraculous healings and deliverances that were shared after we finished our first "Back to the Roots" seminar in Herisau, Switzerland. Hanspeter and Anita Vogt had welcomed us, and all the Jews, with open arms.

"The church needs to repent," they said.

One of the testimonies shared by a young woman was very touching.

"I had mental problems," she said, "I could not find my identity. They had cast many demons out of me, but I never got free. As you explained about the roots of our faith and the unbreakable connection between the Jews and the Gentiles, peace came into me, and I was reconciled with my roots. I am free now!"

A few months later, we would hear another powerful testimony. Ana had been brought to the seminar by a friend. She did not want to come because she hated religion. She was running away from God. However, the insistence of her friend won, and she did come.

As the Holy Spirit took over the meeting, I cried under His leading, "Cain where is your brother Abel? The blood of your brother is crying to Me from the ground!"

A spirit of repentance fell on the people. Many fell on the floor weeping uncontrollably, breaking before the LORD, confessing their sins and the sins of their forefathers. Hating the Jews, mocking or persecuting them had been prevalent among Christians. It was almost normal.

Ana could not escape from the LORD anymore. Right there, she repented and became thoroughly born again into the Kingdom of the God of Israel. The reconciliation with the Jews and with the roots also brought her reconciliation with God!

I was awed. As a minister of God, I had been crying for fruit and for true disciples to come forth! I was tired of "decisions." I wanted to see fruitful, powerful disciples. I had never fathomed that preaching on the Jewish roots of our faith would be the key for true disciples. Yet the fruit that was starting to come in had the taste of eternity.

A few months later, during our Annual Feast of Trumpets (Rosh Hashanah) Prophetic Conference, I saw people transformed and deepened in their understanding of God as the revelation hit them that Christians are part of the commonwealth of Israel. Christianity, as the religion we know today, had divorced itself from its Jewish/biblical roots at the time of the Council of Nicaea in AD 325 when Emperor Constantine rose to power in Rome.

Then a few months later, in another one of our conferences in Jerusalem, I saw how God touched American Christians with the revelation that they, too, needed to repent of anti-Semitism (hatred of Jews) and alienation from their Jewish roots.

Dorothy, a minister herself, came weeping to the microphone and said, "I didn't know that I had anti-Semitism. I have always loved the Jews, but then I realized I've always blamed them for killing Christ."

Michael, from California, was present at another one of our meetings on the Mount of Olives. As the Spirit of Repentance was operating, he confessed, "LORD, forgive me for allowing jokes about the Jews and partaking of that mockery even in my family. We have sinned against your people."

Still ringing in my ears were the words of Brother George in England, in 1989, a few months after I had received Yeshua as my Jewish Messiah (Yeshua is Jesus' name in Hebrew, and it means "*salvation*"). I was so happy that He was *ours*, and He had come to the Jews first. I was so happy there was meaning to being a Jew, besides being persecuted and hated all day long. I was excited to realize that all the Christians in the world were now my family. I needed family, as I had lost everything before joining the Kingdom of God.

But George was bothered by my *Jewish manners*. He said with much lack of tolerance and impatience, "Now that you are born again, you must stop being a Jew."

I was shocked! I felt rejected. I went home and took a warm bath for comfort. As I lay in the bathtub, the Spirit of God fell upon me and *put me in intercession*. "Forgive George, LORD. Please have mercy on him and his church..."

By the Spirit, I was pleading before the God of Israel to forgive these Christians who were ignorant of their Jewish roots. Little did I know that this kind of arrogance can cause many to be broken off from the olive tree (Israel).

Behold then the kindness and the severity of God; to those who fell, severity, but to you, God's kindness, if you continue in His kindness; otherwise you also will be cut off.

Romans 11:22

Then my thoughts took me to another more recent memory. Francois Nadler, the director and founder of a Christian music school, had invited me to minister at a two-day conference for the churches in the area of Neuchâtel in the French part of Switzerland. As Francois and the worship team ministered in music, I started to move in a powerful prophetic anointing of the Holy Spirit. The presence of the LORD was awesome.

All of a sudden, the Spirit of God spoke to me.

"Dominiquae, stop everything and call the people to repent of anti-Semitism!"

I was bewildered! I thought to myself, *"I have never done this before, I am Jewish. What if they reject me?"*

The insistent and authoritative voice of the Spirit of God said, "If you do not call them to repentance, you will have no more anointing tonight!"

He refused to pour any more revival on unrepentant hearts.

I obeyed the LORD and called the people to repent of anti-Semitism. About two-thirds of the people present stood up to ask for forgiveness for themselves and their parents and grandparents, for the Holocaust during the second world war and other things.

As a representative of the Jewish people, I forgave them and broke the curse of anti-Semitism off them. The Spirit of God came in and was poured out in wonderful measure. The Presence of Yeshua (Jesus) was so strong by the end of the meeting that I couldn't stand there. He is the King. I needed to bow down before Him, so I slipped through the crowd into the office. I found refuge on the floor under a chair.

All of these things I pondered on that El Al plane from Zurich to Tel Aviv. When it started landing, the Spirit of God answered my original question, "What's the big deal of ministering the roots to the church?"

"It is a matter of life and death," He said. "The church is like a beautiful rose that has been cut off in the garden from its roots. It has survived for two days in a vase with water. But on the third day, it will die unless it is planted and connected back to its roots."

I started weeping. My heart was pierced through and through. If it's a matter of life and death, I am willing to pay the price for the sake of the LORD and His children.

The Scriptures say that a day is like a thousand years to the LORD. It has already been two thousand years since the LORD Yeshua (Jesus) was revealed to Israel, and the church came into being in Jerusalem. They were all Jewish then. Now we are entering into a new era of history. Being reconnected to our roots is a matter of life and death!

...a partial hardening has happened to Israel until the fullness of the Gentiles has come in.

Romans 11:25

CHAPTER TWO

For Your Sake

For the law will go forth from Zion
and the word of the LORD from Jerusalem.

—ISAIAH 2:3B

I T WAS THE SPRING of 1991, and I was about to receive my ordination as a minister and a graduate of *Christ for the Nations International* in Dallas, Texas. My husband, Baruch, and I had left Israel a year before to study and prepare for the ministry there. Due to the love of this school for Israel, we had received working scholarships.

My duty was to man the gymnasium office and to clean the premises, including the toilets.

I remember when dear Raymond from the Alumni department said to me, "With your credentials and your education and knowledge of languages, they will not ask you to clean the toilets here." But here I was cleaning the gymnasium toilets. God was training me to serve and to be willing to serve in every position.

It was at one of these work shifts a year after leaving Israel that I turned to the Father and asked Him a crucial question for my life.

"LORD, why did you bring me to the States without my children? I haven't seen them in a year, and meanwhile, they have gone through the Gulf War without me. I can't raise them by calling them once a week on the telephone!"

My children were very little then. My daughter, Adie, had not yet turned six when I left her to go to Bible school. My son, Yuval, was three years old. They were in the custody of my ex-husband, who had divorced me a few days before I experienced my new birth and God's total forgiveness of my sins through the blood atonement of my Messiah, Yeshua (Jesus). Yet I had the right to see them as often as I wanted.

They had accepted Yeshua into their hearts and they were growing in their faith. Our relationship was becoming closer and closer. Just when everything was starting to fall into place familywise, the LORD called me to leave everything, marry Baruch another Messianic Jew, and go together with him to Bible school.

I obeyed God because I owed Him my very breath. I was very broken when I met Him, and He was my Healer and the Lifter of my soul. So, I left my children behind and went to train for ministry, yet I never asked God, "*Why?*" until that afternoon a year later, just before the ordination ceremony.

"God," I said, "you are mighty and all-powerful. You could have moved heaven and earth for me to be able to bring my children with me, legally. But you had me leave them. Why? I can't raise them with a telephone call once a week, LORD!"

The voice of my Father, the God of Israel, answered clearly in my heart, "It pleased Me to bruise you. I want you to have authority in every place I send you, to tell My children that I miss them, that I can't raise them up when they call Me only once a week."

I felt like a stone. I thought to myself, "Has God chosen me for that?" I couldn't completely understand what He meant. Yet I knew He had spoken, and He would reveal this great mystery to me in due time.

Three and a half years went by as my husband Baruch and I started our traveling ministry. We went to mainland China where the LORD used us to start a work of the Spirit. We risked our lives to preach the gospel in forbidden areas. Their secret police almost arrested us because we were in an area forbidden to foreigners. Nevertheless, alongside the hardship of the roads and the conditions, the LORD confirmed His Word through us. Many people were born again, and some were miraculously healed.

He also took us to the Philippines, where we ministered to the victims of the volcanic eruption of Mount Pinatubo. The prophetic word we spoke brought life to the believers in the area and they decided to stay instead of running away. As they believed God, they started to prosper. Everywhere we went, the power of the Holy Spirit was present and mighty to heal, deliver, save and transform: God was training us.

During that time, we came in contact with prophetic ministries in the United States. We also came in contact with the infamous *replacement theology*, a theology that states, "the church is now Israel, and the Jews have been rejected by God – that Israel is like any other country and the Christians have inherited all of the blessings, and the Jews all of the curses."

We learned a lot from a prophetic ministry in the Florida area. But we couldn't ignore the fact that our very presence as Jews in their midst was uncomfortable to them. We were constantly aware of their fear and suspicion. They were concerned that we might influence some of their people to keep the Jewish Law or the feasts of Israel. They were sorely afraid of the natural and practical application of the Laws of YHVH. During that time, the LORD taught us to eat "spiritual chicken" – enjoy the meat and spit out the bones, enjoy what came from God, and ignore the rest. There were many "bones," though, and occasionally they hurt our throats.

It was the summer of 1993, over three years after we had left our beloved Israel, and we knew the LORD's timing was at hand for us to go back. It was time to start establishing a prophetic work in the land, a work that would minister the Word of the LORD as written by the prophet Isaiah Chapter 2 verse 3b, "For the Law will go forth from Zion and the Word of the LORD from Jerusalem."

The excitement of being able to see my children again was almost more than I could bear. A sister in the church we had been sent out from the Dallas area gave me a word from the LORD.

"Dominiquae, these are going to be hard times, but the LORD has thoroughly prepared you for what is to come. You will be strong enough." *"What does she mean?"* I said to myself. Soon enough, I would have an answer to that question.

During the missions conference of the Full Gospel of Churches and Ministers International—the fellowship to which we were affiliated as ordained ministers—the answer came.

The telephone rang, disturbing the beauty of a summer's day in Baltimore, Maryland. Our pastor was on the line. "Call Israel immediately," he said. "A terrible accident has happened to your ex-husband. Your children need you!"

Only a few days earlier, I had spoken with the father of my children to prepare him for our return in August. He seemed to have softened. I had even asked him about the softening I perceived. He said that as a tour guide, he had guided Messianic Jews, and they were "very nice people," so he could understand things better.

"However," he said, "They all want me to repent and accept Yeshua, but I am not repenting!" He was so emphatic in his tone of voice and so arrogant.

A cold chill pierced my bones as I warned him with sadness, "Please do not be prideful against God."

And now something terrible had happened. I called my ex-husbands family. His father answered and said, "My son has taken his life. He killed himself less than two weeks ago."

My heart froze. "Why didn't you call me?" The freezing, hateful reply, "We are doing everything in our power so that you may never have your children back legally." then he hung up on me.

My ex-husband had had devastating bouts of manic depression in the past: Suicide was one of the predicaments of that condition.

I started weeping and crying in mourning: A destroyed life and two little children who would forever carry the mark of what their dad had done – so much pain for these two little children of mine to suffer!

Automatically, aided by my loving husband, I started packing to return to Israel at once. I knew a bitter legal fight was awaiting me. I knew I needed to maintain my thoughts on the LORD. I had to be thankful amid this distress, thankful that God is my ever-present help in times of trouble. Though, I felt my heart breaking into a million pieces.

Arriving home in Israel was a sad event; I arrived all alone. Baruch had to stay in America for an additional month to organize the practical details of our home going.

My children were hurting and had been cultured to be estranged from me. Their paternal grandparents were very hateful towards me and they communicated that hate to them. They had already taken all the necessary steps to ensure their custody over the children. A bitter battle was ahead of me.

Ringing in my ears were the words of a Jewish prophet who happened to arrive in Dallas from South Africa a couple of days before we returned to Israel. He had never met me before and did not know anything about my situation. Yet he prophesied, "I see two strong hands filled with hate. They are holding your two children. Then I see a pile of legal papers. They have done everything in their power for you to not ever have your children back. I see the LORD Jesus; He is standing next to an open door and He is smiling. He says, 'There is nothing you can do to bring your children back. But I am fighting for you and I will bring you back your children.'"

I battled in the courts of Israel for a year and a half. During that time, I was allowed to see the children once a week. Most of the visits were under the supervision of social workers. It was a time of deep distress for me. Yet God gave me the grace to stand and to resist bitterness. He gave me the love for all my enemies.

I still recall how, at the first court meeting, the prosecutor presented before the judge all the evidence against me. On top of all the legal papers was my testimony of salvation. I had written it after I accepted my Messiah. In that testimony, I exposed my sins and the forgiving power of the LORD. Today that testimony is out on the market; my book called "YES!"

The prosecutor said, "If you want to know about Dominiquae, all the evidence against her is here, written in her own hand."

My testimony of salvation was the evidence against me! Something inside of me shouted, "Hallelujah!" for in the book of Revelation 12:11, it is written, "And they overcame him (the devil), because of the blood of the lamb and because of the word of their testimony and they did not love their lives even to death."

While the judge, lawyers, psychologists, and social workers of the Israeli courts read my testimony of salvation, I felt God was accomplishing far beyond what I could see. Deep within me, though, I knew the way out was not going to come through the courts. And indeed, in December of 1994, one and half years later, the judge pronounced the verdict. "Custody over the children Adie and Yuval is denied to the mother. No official visiting rights are given besides those that the local social worker would allow."

My husband was devastated; he had stood with me and had seen the injustice of the whole process. He had seen my agony. Yet, somehow, I had total peace about it. I did not feel defeated but victorious. I knew deep within my heart that this verdict, for the time being, was God's will for me. I knew that what He had promised, He would accomplish in His own timing and without my help.

Something inside my heart also told me, *"I have work to do."*

Right after the court battle ended, I found myself traveling extensively in ministry. Many doors in many countries were opening up. The message that was stirring in me was the message that God had brought me forth for, "Call my children to come back to Me. Call them to come back to their roots!"

One day I was praying and meditating upon the things that had happened to me with my children when God asked me a question.

"Dominiquae, what would happen if I returned your children to you right now? Would you be able to travel to the nations and preach?"

I answered, "Surely if my children came back to me now, they would be very demanding of my attention and I could not be free to go to the nations in the same manner. Caring for them would totally consume my time."

The LORD said something then that I will never forget. And I pray that you, the reader, will allow your heart to be pierced with the power of His statement.

"In the same way that you left your children behind in order to go to minister to the Gentiles, so I had to leave My Jewish children behind to call the Gentiles to the Kingdom. I had to forsake them and harden them for a season to call in the Gentiles. In the same manner that your heart is aching over your wounded children who have been estranged from you, so I am aching for My Jewish children who are estranged from Me. In the same manner that your children felt bitter because you abandoned them, my Jewish children feel abandoned by Me, so they cannot believe in My goodness."

He continued, "Now go and tell the Christians that I call them to repentance and to lay down their lives for their Jewish brothers. Tell them that I am coming soon, and this is the time to comfort My Jewish children and to call them unto Me. Tell them also that this is the end of the times of the Gentiles, and that is why I send you to urge them to come back to their roots and the love of Israel."

A Time of Repentance

Dear child of God, if you have read until now and you already feel moved to search your heart and repent, please do so now. I believe the following chapters contain many revelations about the identity of the church and the identity of the LORD. However, hearts that contain anti-Semitism, whether in a hidden form or a very obvious one, cannot receive God's revelation and God's healing. I ask you to open your heart and to be honest with yourself and with the LORD.

Search your heart and ask yourself the following questions.

» Have I hated the Jews?
» Have I blamed them for killing Christ?
» Am I jealous of them?
» Do I have "replacement theology" in me?

» Do I believe that God has 'replaced Israel' and I am now Israel?

» Am I indifferent to the Jews, and to what happens in Israel?

» Have I partaken of derogatory jokes against the Jews?

» Has my family been involved in any Jewish discrimination?

» Have I been arrogant against the Jews?

» Have I extended God's comfort and kindness to them?

» Am I eternally thankful to them for giving us the Bible and Yeshua (Jesus)?

» Am I willing to *answer the call* and lay down my life for them?

Please pray this prayer with me

Heavenly Father, I come before You in humility. I ask You, LORD, to forgive me for any arrogance I have had against Your Jewish people. LORD, I ask You to convict me of my sins and the sins of my ancestors. Take me through a process of repentance, LORD, so I can fulfill Your End time call upon my life and so that all my family can be blessed. Deliver me from ignorance and estrangement from the Jewish/biblical roots of my faith. In the name of Yeshua (Jesus), I pray. Amen!

CHAPTER THREE

The Divorce

"Then Jeroboam built Shechem in the hill country of Ephraim, and lived there. And he went out from there and he built Penuel. And Jeroboam said in his heart, 'Now the kingdom will return to the house of David. If these people go up to offer sacrifices in the house of the LORD at Jerusalem, then the heart of this people will return to their LORD, even to Rehoboam king of Judah; and they will kill me and return to Rehoboam king of Judah.' So the king consulted, and made two golden calves and he said to them, 'It is too much for you to go up to Jerusalem; behold your gods, O Israel, that brought you up from the land of Egypt.' And he set one in Bethel and the other he put in Dan. Now this thing became a sin, for the people went to worship before the one as far as Dan. And he made houses on the high places, and made priests from among all the people who were not of the sons of Levi. And Jeroboam instituted a feast in the eighth month on the fifteenth day of the month, like the feast which is in Judah, and he went up to the altar; thus he did in Bethel, sacrificing to the calves which he had made. Then he went up to the altar which he had made in Bethel on the fifteenth day of the eighth month, even in the month which he had devised in his own heart; and he instituted a feast for the sons of Israel, and went up to the altar to burn incense."

—1 KINGS 12:25-33

T HE FOLLOWING EXCERPT IS from the letter of the Emperor (Constantine) to all those not present at the Council of Nicaea (found in Eusebius, Vita Const. Lib III 18-20).

When the question relative to the sacred festival of Easter arose, it was universally thought that it would be convenient that all should keep the feast on one day; for what could be more beautiful and more desirable than to see this festival, through which we receive the hope of immortality, celebrated by all with one accord and in the same manner? It was declared to be particularly unworthy for this, the holiest of festivals, to follow the customs (the calculation) of the Jews, who had soiled their hand with the most fearful of crimes, and whose minds were blinded. In rejecting their custom, we may transmit to our descendants the legitimate mode of celebrating Easter, which we have observed from the time of the Savior's passion (according to the day of the week).

We ought not therefore to have anything in common with the Jew, for the Savior has shown us another way our worship following a more legitimate and more convenient course (the order of the days of the week). And consequently, in unanimously adopting this mode, we desire, dearest brethren, to separate ourselves from the detestable company of the Jew. For it is truly shameful for us to hear them boast that without their direction we could not keep this feast. How can they be in the right, they who, after the death of the Savior, have no longer been led by reason but by wild violence, as their delusion may urge them? They do not possess the truth in this Easter question, for in their blindness and repugnance to all improvements, they frequently celebrate two Passovers in the same year. We could not imitate those who are openly in error.

How, then, could we follow these Jews who are most certainly blinded by error? For, to celebrate a Passover twice in one year is totally inadmissible.

But even if this were not so, it would still be your duty not to tarnish your soul by communication with such wicked people (the Jews). You should consider not only that the number of churches in these provinces make a majority, but also that it is right to demand what our reason approves, and that we should have nothing in common with the Jews.[*]

During the second and third centuries, the Christian church fathers unleashed a cruel discriminatory campaign against the Jews and anything Jewish, including the Torah – the Law of Moses.

In his book *Our Father Abraham*, Marvin Wilson states on pg. 94:

---

[*] Eusebius, *Vita Const.* Lib III 18-20

"Furthermore the Church Fathers taught that the unfaithfulness of the Jewish people resulted in a collective guilt which made them subject to the permanent curse of God."

Among the biggest persecutors were Justin Martyr and Origen, but there are many other well-known names as well.

In the year AD 325, Constantine adopted Christianity as the official religion of the Eastern Roman Empire called Byzantium. He made official what had already started happening in the second and third centuries—the total divorce from the Jews and anything connected with them, including the Law of Moses. It was at that time what we call the "New Testament" was canonized. Until then, the only Scriptures were the Tanakh (Old Testament).

One of the characteristics of the Constantine Era is that Constantine changed the biblical seasons and feasts. He also set himself to be the head of the state church.

Constantine was a sun worshiper till the day of his death. He was never born again, and yet the whole church fell into his trap. In the book of Daniel (Daniel 7:25), we read that the anti-Christ will change the times and the seasons. In this, Constantine was a type of anti-Christ. He forbade the celebration of Passover and instead instituted Easter, a feast and a name derived from the Babylonian goddess, Ishtar. He also changed the day of rest to Sunday instead of the Shabbat** because he was a sun worshiper who worshiped his god, the Sun, on the Sun-day.

The entire church fell into his trap because Constantine commanded the persecution against Christians to cease. Until then, believers were being thrown to the lions for their faith.

** Pronounced Sha-bat where *a* is like the *a* in "father." Translated Sabbath in English. The seventh day of the week starting at sundown on Friday and going until sundown on Saturday. Each day begins with the evening – see Genesis 1. The day God rested after Creation – Genesis 2:1-3. 4th Commandment – see Exodus 20:8-11

Persecution was tremendously fierce during the time of the Roman Empire. So, when Constantine declared a "peace treaty," the believers, exhausted from persecution, welcomed this "peace treaty" and thus compromised their faith. This compromise has cost the lives of far more people than if the persecution had continued.

The Constantine state church is affecting Christianity to this very day. It is deceiving many people, who are worshiping dead saints and idols and statues of Mary, into believing that they are saved. Yet the LORD says in Deuteronomy 5:8–9 and Exodus 20:5 that the sin of idolatry is visited upon the third or fourth generation.

On top of that, the hatred for the Jews institutionalized by Constantine has given birth to monstrous events such as the Spanish Inquisition, the bloody Crusades, and the Nazi Holocaust. Every one of these massacres against Jews was propagated in the name of Christ and the Cross. Countless deceived people are burning in hell right now because of their hatred for the Jews as branches who have been "cut off" because of their arrogance (Romans 11:18-22).

It is interesting to mention that a very similar thing happened to the Northern tribes of Israel during the ninth to eighth century B.C. Because of the sins of King Solomon, who went into idolatry, the Kingdom of Israel divided into two kingdoms: The Kingdom of Judah in the south, and the Kingdom of Israel, also called *Ephraim*, in the north. The king of Ephraim was Jeroboam. Jeroboam was not from the kingly lineage of David. He feared to lose the ten tribes who were under his rule. So, he replaced the temple worship with idol worship, he replaced the Mosaic Law, including the feasts, with human-made feasts. He divorced the Northern tribes of Israel from their roots in the same way that Constantine officially divorced the church from its Jewish roots, replacing the feasts and the Law with *pagan* customs.

Because of the sin of Jeroboam, God rejected Ephraim or
the kingdom of Israel from being His people and sowed them
into the nations. "... for I will no longer have compassion on
the house of Israel that I will ever forgive them. But I will have
compassion on the house of Judah" (Hosea 1:6-7).

Constantine's sin of divorcing the church from its Jewish
roots I will name, "the sin of Jeroboam in the church."

The sin of Jeroboam led to the total rejection of God by the
northern tribes as depicted in 2 Kings.

**So the Lord was very angry with Israel and removed them
from His sight; none was left except the tribe of Judah (the
Jewish people of today).**

2 Kings 17:18

The sin of Jeroboam in the church can have the same outcome, as God said that He would reject those who are arrogant
towards the "natural branches," the Jews. Therefore, repenting
of the sin of Jeroboam in the church is a matter of life or death.

The divorce from the Jews and the Jewish roots of the faith
have born children of disobedience, ignorance, Lawlessness,
and paganism. The Bible says, "a false prophet is recognized by
his fruit." (Matthew 7:15–16). The fruit of institutionalized
Christianity has been murder, hatred, and massacres (Crusades,
the Spanish Inquisition, Nazi Holocaust). But what about
Protestants and Spirit-filled Christians?

Martin Luther was greatly used by God in the 16th century to
restore the church from the Dark Ages—caused by the divorce
from the Jews and the Jewish biblical roots—to the original
truth of salvation by grace through faith. In the beginning, he
tried to win the Jews to the Lord as he understood that they

were still the people of God and that the Gentile Christians had alienated them.

However, the Jews by then had suffered several Crusades and the Spanish Inquisition. They rejected Luther's attempts to win them over to the gospel. Due to that, Luther became bitter and developed a vehement hatred towards the Jews. He issued a series of articles and pamphlets, including *On the Jews and their Lies*. In these, he labeled the Jews as "venomous," "thieves," and "disgusting vermin."

He had a real problem with the Law to the point that he wanted to leave the book of James out of the New Testament because it said, "faith without works is dead" (James 2:20 KJV).

The seed of hatred and anti-Semitism was transmitted through Luther to all Protestant Christians. The "arrogance of the branches" and the sin of Jeroboam in the church continued its destructive course to this very day!

A new reformation is knocking at the doors of the church: *Go back to the roots!*

CHAPTER FOUR

The Torah

And then I will declare to them, 'I NEVER KNEW YOU;
DEPART FROM ME, YOU WHO PRACTICE LAWLESSNESS.'

—MATTHEW 7:23

T HIS SCRIPTURE IS VERY strong, especially because it is spoken to those who are believers, even those casting out demons. They know the power of God. We can't just ignore it and spiritualize it. It is better to be shocked out of complacency than to receive this terrible "greeting" from the LORD when we arrive at heaven's gates.

The word "law" is interchangeable with "Torah." By saying "Torah," I mean only the five books of Moses; those regulations and instructions that were given to Israel by God Himself. Nearly every chapter in Leviticus and Deuteronomy begins with, "And the LORD spoke to Moses saying, speak to the children of Israel..." I do not mean the Talmud, Kabbalah, or other Rabbinical writings.

To correctly interpret this Scripture in Matthew 7:23, we need to look at it in the light of the Scriptures in Matthew 5.

Do not think that I came to abolish the Law or the Prophets; I did not come to abolish but to fulfill... For truly I say to you, until heaven and earth pass away, not the smallest letter or stroke shall pass away from the Law until all is accomplished.

**Whoever then annuls one of the least of these Command-
ments and so teaches others, shall be called least in the kingdom of heaven; but whoever keeps and teaches them, he shall
be called great in the kingdom of heaven. For I say to you, that
unless your righteousness surpasses that of the scribes and
Pharisees, you shall not enter the kingdom of heaven.**

Matthew 5:17–20

What the LORD is saying here is confirmed in Matthew 7:23
when He tells those who have been *doing* things in His name,
even working miracles, to depart from Him since they have been
without Law, or without *Torah*, which are God's instructions in
righteousness.

Matthew 5:17 has been misinterpreted for many centuries
to say that because the LORD *fulfilled* the Law— (from now
on, I will use the proper Hebrew word, Torah) —then we who
believe in Him are now "free from the Torah."

That, of course, would pose a tremendous threat to the very definition of the New Covenant, as written in Jeremiah 31:31,33 (KJV).

**Behold the days come, saith the LORD, that I will make a
New Covenant with the house of Israel, and with the house
of Judah ... But this shall be the covenant that I will make with
the house of Israel; After those days, saith the LORD, I will
put my Law in their inward parts, and write it in their hearts;
and will be their God, and they shall be my people.**

Jeremiah 31:31,33 KJV

The very definition of the New Covenant is the time when the
Torah is written in the heart rather than on tablets of stone. Just
as the finger of God wrote the First Covenant and the Torah on

the stone tablets in Sinai, the New Covenant happens when the finger of God writes the Torah on the heart of a believer.

The question that remains is, "What does the word 'fulfill' mean?" This word is a normal term that was often used two thousand years ago. Yeshua meant, "Do not think that I came to destroy the Torah or the prophets by misinterpretation, but I came to interpret them to the full." In other words, "I am the only one who can fully interpret and explain all the Laws and all the prophecies. Without Me, you can't have the full understanding!" Then, of course, it would make sense why the LORD continued to give His interpretation of the Torah as we see in the following verses.

For example, look at the verses in Matthew 5:

"Ye have heard that it was said by them of old time, 'Thou shalt not kill ...' But I say unto you, that whosoever is angry with his brother without a cause shall be in danger of the judgment..."

Matthew 5:21–22 KJV

Isn't it clear that Yeshua is interpreting the Torah to the full here? It is not enough to have the correct external actions, but our hearts need to be right as well. Yeshua also said:

"Ye have heard that it was said by them of old time, 'Thou shalt not commit adultery', but I say unto you, that whosoever looketh on a woman to lust after her hath committed adultery with her already in his heart."

Matthew 5:27–28 KJV

Again, it's extremely clear and obvious that Yeshua is fully interpreting the Torah by challenging us not only to keep the external action but also to have our hearts right and pure. An impure heart or impure actions carry the same weight in God's eyes.

From all this we can understand a few things:

1. The Torah is not abolished.
2. The definition of "new covenant" is having the Torah written in our hearts by the finger of God,
3. We need Yeshua to interpret the Torah and the Prophets to the full. Since Yeshua in Hebrew means "salvation," then it can be said we need to be saved to have the full interpretation of Torah and walk in it.

When we get saved, we immediately receive the Holy Spirit, who is the deposit or proof of our salvation (see 1st Corinthians 3:16; 1 John 4:13). The Holy Spirit is the finger of God who writes the Torah on our hearts (see Luke 11:20; Deuteronomy 9:20; Exodus 8:19). The same Spirit by which we cast out devils and heal the sick is the one who writes God's Torah in our hearts. So, the only way for us as believers to walk in obedience to God's Torah is to walk by the Spirit (Romans 8:1-8). Romans 8 says:

Because the carnal mind is enmity against God: for it is not subject to the Law of God, neither indeed can be.

Romans 8:7 KJV

So, the difference between those who walk according to the carnal, fleshly mind that is an enemy of God, and those who walk by the Spirit, is whether we are subject to God's Law or we are not. Those who are not subject in their minds to God's Torah are carnal, and those who are subject to God's Torah are spiritual or Spirit-led.

That, of course, makes sense in the light of the revelation that God's Holy Spirit both interprets and writes the Torah in our hearts. Since we can't have the correct and full interpretation without Yeshua, neither can we understand or walk in the fullness of the Torah without the guidance of the Holy Spirit. In other words, the Holy Spirit is the key for us to understand and obey God's Laws and instructions.

Since our growth in the Spirit is an ongoing process, so is our growth in the understanding and correct application of the Torah. We can't just read the Laws and try to figure out with our own reason how to apply them to our lives. We need the Holy Spirit to teach us and fully interpret those Laws to us continually. That is why the Holy Spirit is called our Teacher—this was the usual term given to the rabbi who taught the Torah and its applications. Now the Spirit of God is our official, God-appointed Torah Teacher (see John 14:16-21, 26).

The LORD calls the Holy Spirit "the Comforter" who will teach us all things. Yeshua goes on to say in John 14:21–26 that the one who loves Him keeps His Words; these Words are not His but are the Words and Commandments of the Father who sent Him. Since Yeshua and the Father are one, Yeshua and the God of Israel have the same set of Commandments. And the proof that we love Yeshua is that *we keep His Commandments* as revealed to us by the Holy Spirit.

I remember that for many years, I sought God on how to keep and relate to the *Shabbat* (Sabbath). Since I fly a lot to minister in different countries, I have prayed for many hours during different flights for God to reveal this Commandment to me, "Thou shalt keep the Sabbath holy." Each time I have had more and more revelation and have been able to obey God, not under the letter of the Law that kills but by the Spirit that gives life (2 Corinthians 3:6).

I have been seeking the Holy Spirit's interpretation to the different Commandments as I want to walk in obedience to God's

Word and not as a "Lawless" or "Torahless" one. God has been gracious and patient with me in my growth in understanding His Commandments. I believe that as you seek Him for yourself with a genuine heart, He will do the same for You.

I must warn you here against two extreme and incorrect reactions to the Torah.

1. Believers who hear the message on the Torah and feel guilty that they have not been obeying it, "put fig leaves on" and try to "cover their guilt" by doing everything religiously without the fully correct interpretation by the Holy Spirit. These believers miss it because they do not have an intimate relationship with the Holy Spirit who is the only one who can interpret the Law for us. They fall into religiosity and "doing works" without the Spirit. This is how a cultic spirit develops.

2. On the other hand, there are other believers especially among the theologically schooled who act violently to the message on Torah with a deep fear that "people will come under the Law." They then fall prey to the trap of teaching people not to keep the Torah because it is all fulfilled and thus irrelevant for the believers in the New Covenant. The danger of that is pretty serious since the LORD says in Matthew 5:19 (KJV), "Whosoever therefore shall break one of these least Commandments, and shall teach men so, he shall be called the least in the kingdom of heaven."

Both of these reactions are incorrect, harmful and in need of repentance.

May I suggest that you stop here and pray and seek your heart before you go any further?

Dear heavenly Father, I would like to have a pure heart before You concerning the Torah. I pray that You give me the full in-

terpretation of Your Laws through the Holy Spirit. I purpose
to seek Your face on this issue and I humble myself to hear from
You. In Yeshua's Name. Amen.

One of the major outcomes of the divorce from the Jewish
roots was the problem of dealing with the Old Testament. In
an attempt to keep the Old Testament as part of the Bible, the
church fathers decided that the way to interpret it would be to
allegorize and spiritualize it. Thus, the Law could be spiritualized, and all mention of Israel would mean the church, and
Jerusalem would mean the New Jerusalem and so on. The Law,
of course, was done away with at the Cross – or so they taught.

This problem continues to this day as we cannot reconcile
Old Testament scriptures to New Testament scriptures. Take,
for example, scriptures that talk about all mankind coming to
bow down before the LORD from Shabbat to Shabbat from
New Moon to New Moon. Since the Law was "obsolete" and
Constantine had changed the Shabbat from Saturday to Sunday,
this Scripture in Isaiah 66:22–24 was interpreted to mean from
Sunday to Sunday.

**And it shall come to pass, that from one new moon to another
and from one sabbath to another, shall all flesh come to worship before me, saith The LORD.**

Isaiah 66:23.

It is quite clear that all people will worship God forever on the
Shabbat. Nothing in the Scriptures even hints that God would
change the Shabbat to Sunday.

I personally believe we should worship God every day of the
week. But from Friday night to Saturday night is Shabbat and
it is the special day God Himself chose to be worshiped for

all eternity. It is also the fourth of the Ten Commandments, "Remember the sabbath day, to keep it holy" (Exodus 20:8).

It is very interesting to note that in the last few years, many congregations started "prophetic meetings" or "School of the Holy Spirit" meetings on Friday nights. Those meetings are normally the most anointed ones and the presence of the Holy Spirit is considerably stronger. That is no coincidence. On Friday night begins the Shabbat. Most Jewish homes are celebrating it and setting it apart with a festive family meal. At the same time Yeshua has come to celebrate His Shabbat with His redeemed ones who have been "grafted into the olive tree" (Romans 11) by sharing with them a special "festive meal" in His Presence.

I was leading a prayer meeting for women at one time. As the Holy Spirit was moving greatly in our midst, many physical and emotional healings were happening. A young lady in her thirties came to the meeting for the first time. She asked me to pray for her. She was suffering from heart problems and was taking a lot of medication. I took one look at her and asked her one question, "Do you keep the Shabbat?" (Shabbat actually means "to go on strike" and stop all regular work). To which she answered, "Of course I do not keep the Shabbat. I am a student and I need money for my studies. So, I work seven days a week!" I just said to her, "Repent before God for breaking the Shabbat and you will be healed!" Before I finished the sentence she was on the floor weeping and crying for violating His loving Laws and instructions to us, His Creation. She got thoroughly healed and did not have to take any more heart medication.

We need to continually remember that the Shabbat and all the other biblical, Jewish feasts were already set at the time of Creation. Therefore, they are still very relevant, "And God said let there be lights in the firmament of the heaven to divide the day from the night; and let them be for signs and for seasons and for days and years" (Genesis 1:14, KJV). The same word used for the feasts of God or holy convocations in Leviticus 23:2 is used in Genesis 1:14 for seasons. That word is moadim. It means "testimonials" or "rehearsals." And indeed, as we celebrate the Shabbat and all the other holy biblical festivals we get to rehearse and give testimony of God as a Creator and as a Redeemer. (Please also read Isaiah 56:6–8).

Concerning the dietary Laws, we often misquote the scripture, 1 Timothy 4:4–5, "For everything created by God is good, and nothing is to be rejected, if it is received with gratitude; for it is sanctified by means of the Word of God and prayer." We often paraphrase it like this, "We are to eat anything as long as we pray over it." We totally ignore that it needs to be sanctified by the Word of God and prayer. The only Word that Paul was referring to and that Timothy had available to him, was the Tanakh (Old Testament). The New Testament had not been compiled yet.

The Word never sanctifies pigs or snakes or shellfish for human consumption. The animals have never changed. God created some for human consumption and called them "clean," and some not for human consumption and called them "unclean" (Leviticus11). Noah, who lived before the Law was given, knew about this. So, he brought into the ark of the clean animals seven by seven (to eat and to sacrifice to the LORD) and of the unclean animals only two by two (Genesis 7:2).

Also, many people interpret the vision Peter had on the roof in the city of Jaffa to say that God was cleansing all animals; but that is not the interpretation of the vision:

While he was wondering what the vision meant, "... the Spirit said to him, 'Behold three men are looking for you, but arise, go downstairs and accompany them without misgivings for I

have sent them Myself" (Acts10:19–20). When he arrived at
Caesarea at the house of Cornelius, Peter said to them, "You
yourselves know how unlawful it is for a man who is a Jew to
associate with a foreigner or to visit him; and yet God has shown
me that I should not call any man common or unclean" (Acts
10:28). How did God show him that? A sheet with clean and
unclean animals descended three times and three Gentile men
came to meet him as he was wondering what the vision meant.

If we do a scientific test on the animals, we will find out that
they are basically the same as two thousand years ago. However,
there is a very clear difference between born again people and
people who have not yet received the blood atonement of Yeshua.
The LORD cleanses people by His blood sacrifice, not by animals.
Now both Jews and Gentiles have access to God through the
blood of the Messiah and by the same Spirit, the Holy Spirit.

Please understand what I'm saying. Your salvation does not
depend on the animals you eat. But breaking the Laws of the
LORD (even if it is because of ignorance) harms us physically,
mentally and spiritually.

The LORD fulfilled all of the requirements of the Law to pur-
chase our righteousness, so that we can obey Him, not by our
own strength, but by the strength of the Spirit who He has given
us. That same Spirit who raised Yeshua from the dead dwells in us.

He is our Teacher and Counselor. He will write God's Laws
on our hearts. But how can He do that if we do not allow Him
to because our doctrines tell us that "we are free from the Law"
and "the Law is bondage and slavery"! It is far greater slavery to
suffer the consequences of violating God's Law and principles,
whether they are moral, social or dietary. He is just knocking on
the door of our hearts to let Him write His Law on our hearts!

I still remember when we were in Florida and a ministry couple wanted to receive nutritional counseling from me. These were very busy and famous ministers of the LORD. Both of them were overweight and they traveled a bit. So, they needed a radical change in nutrition. In the past, I used to be a health consultant and nutritionist, which is why they thought it a good idea to take some counseling from me on how to eat. They made an appointment. But a few days later they canceled it because of a sudden ministry engagement. I was sorry because I felt their health was in jeopardy.

A few days later we heard that they and their daughter who was with them were at the hospital due to a violent attack of food poisoning. They were very sick! On the way back from their ministry engagement, they stopped at an "All You Can Eat" shrimp place and they got violently sick from the shrimp they ate.

If they would have come to the nutritional counseling appointment, I would have told them about the dietary Laws as written in Leviticus 11. I would have told them that there is a difference between clean and unclean animals; that shellfish and shrimp have not been created for human consumption... that they are the vacuum cleaners of the ocean and, because of that, they are prone to cause many diseases. The same with pork. The pig has no sweat glands. Therefore, it rolls in the mud to cool itself down. It eats garbage and it cannot get rid of its poisons. People who know how to cook pork know not to boil pork for too long because all the poisons trapped within the pork come to the surface. It is a well-known fact in nutrition that pork and all its derivatives are harmful to the arteries because of their high fat content.

Once my husband and I were preaching in Colombia about the Torah and the dietary Laws. A woman seemed to be so excited that she could not contain herself. As we asked her about it, she said, "I am a doctor in Microbiology and I have been doing autopsies on different populations. I have seen that Jewish people who keep the dietary Laws have a far healthier intestinal environment and far less bacteria than normal Christians who do not keep the dietary Laws. I have also found that many Christians die from very virulent bacteria that have no cure and Jewish people don't suffer from them. Also, there is a horrible disease that looks like epilepsy, but it is not. It's a disease that happens to people who eat pork."

Later we ministered to the leadership and staff of that church and gave an altar call for people to repent from breaking God's Torah. Many people fell under the power of God and rose up refreshed or healed. Among them was a woman who was crying profusely. She confessed that her child had this epileptic-like disease from eating pork because she had been feeding it to him since he was a baby, thinking it to be nutritious! The mother repented, and we prayed for the healing of her child.

In another circumstance, we were ministering in the Far East to a pastor who moved very strongly in the power and anointing of God. He confided in us that he could not sleep for more than three hours at night. I told him to stop eating shellfish and unclean seafood as they cause a toxin build-up in the body and they are not fit for human consumption. Since God had previously spoken to him about the pork being unclean, he decided to go further in obeying God's Torah. Two months later we met again, and he said to me, "Dominiquae, you're not going to believe this: I am sleeping seven hours a night." He definitely looked like a different person.

During the time when the Black Plague swept through Europe, people were dying like flies. The only ones who were still healthy were the Jews because they obeyed the "dietary Laws" written in Leviticus 11. Of course, the Jews were blamed for the plague because they were the only ones to be protected from it.

God has no shadow of turning in Him. But since the divorce from the biblical roots, it *appears* to be that God has changed His mind on many issues.

Yet the wisdom of God is all-encompassing. His Word is indeed a lamp unto our feet and a light unto our path. The LORD says in Hosea 4:6 that His people are perishing for lack of knowledge. We can see evidence of that everywhere, especially in the long lines for healing in the church! People come to get healed of the same conditions again and again. But if they would give heed to our manual of instruction, the Torah (Law), instead of their own understanding, they would be a healthier people!

Another Law that is largely ignored, one that in our "freedom" we constantly violate, is the "Niddah Law." It is written in Leviticus 15:19 not to have sex with your wife during the time of her monthly period and to abstain from intercourse for seven days. I believe many of the feminine diseases, such as miscarriages, cervical cancer, endometriosis and hysterectomies are related to the violation of this statute. Could it be that it is connected with having intercourse during the monthly period? It is well known that we should let the uterus and vagina rest at that time. Also, God being such a wonderful Father knows that a period of necessary abstinence fuels the marriage with renewed desire and love.

In Acts 15:29, there were four Laws given to the Gentiles to apply to their lives immediately after accepting the Messiah. One of these Laws was to abstain from blood. That, of course, includes eating blood and having intercourse at the time of blood, which is the menstrual period.

Many people also misinterpret Paul's writings because they "think Gentile" instead of "thinking Jewish." We cannot understand Paul's writings without understanding his background as a student of the Torah. Paul would never have encouraged anyone to break the Torah. If he had done so, he would have contradicted the words of Yeshua Himself:

"Whoever then annuls one of the least of these Commandments, and so teaches others, shall be called least in the kingdom of heaven; but whoever keeps and teaches them, he shall be called great in the kingdom of heaven."

Matthew 5:19

Which "Commandments" was Yeshua talking about? He was obviously continuing the line of teaching of the previous two verses, "Do not think that I came to abolish the Law or the Prophets." Was Yeshua confused? Was Paul in rebellion to the words of his Master? Not so! But the Gentilized church has interpreted Paul's writings very wrongly.

Yes! Salvation is by grace through faith. Not one of the works of the Law can save us!

But when we receive the New Birth a process begins; the LORD starts writing His Laws in our hearts by the Holy Spirit. This is the process of sanctification (see Jeremiah 31:31–33). In Ephesians 5:26 Paul states about the church, "that He might sanctify her, having cleansed her by the washing of water with the Word." Which word is Paul referring to? The Old Testament, of course. It was the only Word that all the disciples had available. For over three hundred years the church had only the Old Testament Scriptures (Tanakh) to guide them.

When Constantine came to power, he and the church fathers canonized the New Testament in the fourth century. In 2 Timothy 3:16 Paul says to Timothy, "All Scripture is inspired by God and profitable for teaching, for reproof, for correction, for training in righteousness." "All Scripture" means the Torah and the Prophets and the Writings. The name is not "Old Testament"; this is a later terminology used by the divorced church. The name is TaNaKh which is an acronym for Torah (Law), Nevi'im (Prophets), Ketuvim (the Writings as in Psalms, Ecclesiastes, etc.) The word Torah means instruction which is exactly the word Paul uses in 2 Timothy 3:16. He calls it, "instruction in righteousness," in other words, the Torah, also known as the Law, is our instruction in righteousness.

Dear friends, ignoring the Law does not make it go away. There are consequences to our ignorance. It causes us to die for lack of knowledge. It can be likened to a person deciding to defy the law of gravity. Let's say that in order to prove the point, he went to the roof of a tall building and "jumped down by faith." Guess the outcome? He would, of course, crash and most likely die.

This is what the divorce from our Jewish/biblical roots does: we are constantly defying the Laws of the LORD because of ignorance and misinterpretation.

Our faith becomes presumption instead of solid faith based on His Word. When we are ignorant of God's Word, thinking that the Law is abolished, we turn a deaf ear to the Holy Spirit and resist Him all the way! Our mindset stands as a block in our relationship with God.

I am a firm believer that the only way to please the Father is to be led by the Spirit, to be totally under the control and guidance of the Holy Spirit. That is the way Yeshua walked and that is the only way to live an abundant life. Trying to keep the Torah by our own strength is futile. The opposite and correct response is of allowing the Holy Spirit to write the Torah in our hearts. Paul says, "... that the requirement of the Law might be fulfilled in us, who do not walk according to the flesh, but according to the Spirit" (Romans 8:4).

I remember that before I married my husband, I had received numerous visions and words from God about His will for me to marry Baruch. I was so wounded from previous relationships and so afraid of making a mistake that I "fought the devil" for three months, thinking he was deceiving me into the wrong marriage. One day as I was resisting these visions in prayer, I became violently sick. Then I understood I had been resisting the Holy Spirit. As I repented, I became well again.

In the same manner, our church doctrines and mindsets prevent us from yielding to the Holy Spirit. Let's say the Holy Spirit will tell you to stop celebrating Christmas and instead to celebrate the feasts of the LORD as written in the Bible (these are also called Jewish feasts and Jesus celebrated them). Would you yield immediately to the leading of the Spirit? Or would you resist Him for quite a while? Or let's say you are a missionary and are trained to "eat everything that is set before you." How ready would you be to respond to the prompting of the Holy Spirit if He would lead you to eat only "clean animals"? Would you fight against a "spirit of legalism" trying to possess you? Or would you recognize God's own Spirit?

It is interesting to know that when people accept the LORD and have no teaching from the prevailing church doctrines, they often have a very wholesome understanding of the Law. Once we were preaching in the Philippines in a mountainous area to a new congregation. The people there are very simple. The new babes in the LORD did not have much contact with church doctrine. As we taught a seminar on Covenant and on the roots, saying that the dietary Laws were still for today, the people had no problem receiving it.

In fact, one old man by the name of Nicomedes, who had been bitten twice by poisonous snakes (cobras), just believed the Word in Luke 10:19 that God has given us authority to trample on snakes and scorpions and that nothing would harm us. He just said, "God, your word is true; now heal me!" The man was instantly healed. In the same way, when he read that pork was an unclean animal, he took it literally and stopped eating pork. It was a simple thing for him as he walked in "child-like faith," obeying his loving Father and His Torah. He was never taught that the Law was obsolete or that the "Old Testament" needs to be "spiritualized" and "allegorized." He was walking in the Spirit, "not fulfilling the lust of the flesh."

However, in other more urbanized areas of the Philippines, people had been exposed to a lot of "Gentilized Christian doctrine." They had a real tough time receiving the word of truth. For example, it is written in Acts 15:29 to abstain from blood. Many of these Philippine Christians were eaters of blood soup and other "local delicacies." They felt that if they prayed over it, it would be sanctified. God does not sanctify what His Word does not sanctify! Many of "the blood eaters" had trouble in their spiritual walk with the LORD. We had to pray and break the spirit of addiction to blood in them. In Leviticus 17:11 it is written, "For the life of the soul is in the blood." The life of the animal is in its blood and the LORD forbids us to touch it and to partake of the soul of the animal.

I still remember very vividly a magazine we received a few years ago. It was the magazine of one of the most flourishing churches in the Far East. One of the stories caught my attention.

The Head Overseer of this church had gone to Africa to minister to a tribe. The chief of the tribe invited him to partake of their "sacred, covenant meal." It was milk mixed with animal blood. This pastor wanted to win the chief to the LORD. So, he drank blood with him! Then he became violently sick! This meal was certainly not sanctified by the Word! But what shocked me is that the story was written in order to boast of the courage of this pastor who was willing to become sick for the sake of the gospel!

This is the kind of ignorance that is killing us. We have forgotten the Law of our God and in Hosea 4:6, He says, "Since you have forgotten the Law of your God, I also will forget your children."

My husband and I used to lead an outreach on the streets of central Dallas, Texas. It was in an area called "Deep Ellum." This area was plagued with witchcraft, occult, punk rock, new age, homosexuality, skinheads, bikers and Neo Nazis. The human scene there was terrible. For the most part these were young people 20 to 30 years of age. And many of them, if not most of them, were children of Christian families (Catholic, Baptist, Pentecostal, Presbyterian, etc.) cut off from their Jewish/biblical roots. These children were in deep distress. They were being killed by the ignorance in the church and by their lack of identity.

When we cut ourselves off from the Jewish roots of our faith we lose our identity in the same way the 10 tribes of Israel lost their identity when Jeroboam cut them off from the roots and from Temple Worship in Jerusalem (1 Kings 25–33).

One of the most prevalent things we saw was a repeat of the German scene from the 30's as Hitler started recruiting Nazi youth for his purposes. Many of these young people in the Deep Ellum scene in Dallas hated Jews. They believed Jews could never receive God's salvation and forgiveness. We preached the gospel and loved them, and they accepted us. They could not believe we were Jews and we were saved!

In order for these children to be saved, their families needed to repent of anti-Semitism and for repudiating everything Jewish, including the Tanakh. In Proverbs 28:9 we read, "He who turns his ear from listening to the Law, even his prayer is an abomination." We need to learn to repent for our ancestors and break down before God so the curse is removed, and we can have our children back from the dead!

Romans 11:15 gives us a promise: "For if their (the Jews') rejection be the reconciliation of the world what will their acceptance be but life from the dead?" Accepting the Jews and the Jewish biblical roots back is a matter of life and death!

A Prayer of Repentance

Please pray this prayer in order to start the cleansing process of your family tree:

Dear Father in heaven, my ancestors and I have sinned against You and against Your people. We have lived disconnected from our Jewish roots. We have thought that the Law is obsolete, and we have not allowed you to write it on our hearts. We have been afraid of being under the Law, but instead we have gone into Lawlessness. Our children are hurting because of our ignorance of our roots. We ask You to cleanse us from any ignorance of our Jewish roots. We renounce any anti-Semitism in our family, and we bind any familiar spirit of Jewish hatred, of Lawlessness, and of rebellion against the Word of God in the Tanakh. LORD, I ask You to write the Torah in my heart and to sanctify me by Your Word. Please reconnect me and my family with the

Jewish roots of our faith and save our children. Father, I accept the Jews and the biblical roots of our faith back into my heart. Thank You that this will bring resurrection life to me and to my family. In the name of Yeshua, I pray. Amen.

Any problems with this chapter? Read the epilogue now!

Chapter Five

The Fullness of the Gentiles

For I do not want you, brethren, to be uninformed of this mystery—so that you will not be wise in your own estimation—that a partial hardening has happened to Israel until the fullness of the Gentiles has come in; and so all Israel will be saved; just as it is written, "The Deliverer will come from Zion, He will remove ungodliness from Jacob."

—Romans 11:25-26

I N THESE NEXT FEW chapters I will address the issue of the identity of the church. It is a very well-known fact in Psychology that people who are estranged from their real identity, or from their family roots, have many more problems in life than people who know where they belong. One of the major problems of a lack of belonging is rejection. While ministering inner healing or deliverance, I encounter the issue of rejection as a root issue and root cause of most of the emotional problems of God's children. Undoubtedly, many of them suffer from restlessness and a lack of inner peace. They dress really nice with Sunday dresses and make up and a plastic smile, but deep within many are hurting. And they don't understand why. They have heard countless times that Yeshua is the lover of their souls and they are fully accepted in Him; yet rejection and alienation and some emptiness still persist.

I once met a very successful minister who had often ministered in the power of the Holy Spirit to hundreds of thousands of people. He had been a vessel greatly used of God to oversee many churches, and many miracles had happened under his ministry. Yet inside he was nothing but a restless child who could not find his identity in the LORD. He had not "come home" yet and there was an emptiness in him that nothing could fill.

The disconnection from the Jewish roots, and, through that, from the Tanakh, has brought us to a place of "spiritual schizophrenia." It is impossible to fully reconcile the God of Grace with the God of Judgment, the New with the Old. That causes great confusion and the sense that we can't trust God fully because we do not know who He is.

Is He a God of wrath? Is He a gentleman? Is He our Judge? Is He our Father? Is the church something that just happened unrelated to the prophecies of God to Israel? Is the church Israel? If so, who are the Jews? Are they also Israel? If so, is God then marrying two brides: The church and Israel? Is God a bigamist? If He is, how can I trust Him? And if He gave Israel up, how can I trust Him not to give up on me? Am a Jew by faith? Am I a Christian? What's a Christian?

In order to start answering all these questions and bring sanity to our identity problem and health to our souls and spirits, let me give you some interesting figures. The word Israel is mentioned 2,601 times in the Bible. The word *Christian* is mentioned only twice! After the word for God and LORD, Israel is the most often mentioned word in the Bible!

In Revelation 21:10–27, the LORD presented the New Jerusalem, the Bride of the Lamb, to John. "It had a great and high wall, with twelve gates, and at the gates twelve angels; and names were written on them, which are those of the twelve tribes of the sons of Israel ... And the walls of the city had twelve foundation stones, and on them were the twelve names of the twelve apostles of the Lamb."

The gates are Israeli. The foundation stones are all Jewish, because the twelve apostles of the Lamb are all Jewish. If we say that "the sons of Israel" means the church, what do we do then with the rebirth of the Jewish nation in their own land – Israel? And what do we do with the Scripture that heads this chapter? It says that the fullness of the Gentiles will come in, and also that all of Israel will be saved, that is, the "natural branches." So, in order to understand the Bride, we need to understand the "fullness of the Gentiles" and the difference between them and all of Israel.

The first time this terminology, the "fullness of the Gentiles" is used is in the book of Genesis, when Jacob is adopting the two sons of Joseph, Manasseh and Ephraim, as he lays his hands on them before his death. "But Israel stretched out his right hand and laid it on the head of Ephraim, who was the younger, and his left hand on Manasseh's head, crossing his hands, although Manasseh was the first born ... When Joseph saw that his father laid his right hand on Ephraim's head, it displeased him ... And Joseph said to his father, 'Not so my father, for this one is the first-born. Place your right hand on his head.' But his father refused and said, 'I know, my son, I know; he also shall become a people and he also shall be great. However, his younger brother shall be greater than he, and his descendants shall become a fullness of nations'" (Genesis 48:14-19).

The term used here translated "fullness of nations" is in the Hebrew original, *meloh hagoyim*; it is the same term used in Romans 11:25 for "the fullness of the Gentiles" that needs to come in. In Hebrew, the word goyim means "Gentiles" or "nations."

The background of Ephraim is very revealing. He was the second son of Joseph and Osnat. Osnat was an Egyptian, a Gentile. They had born their children in exile, outside of the Land of Israel. So, Ephraim was a child of a mixed marriage. He was adopted by Jacob (Israel) as his very own as he said to Joseph, "And now your two sons, who were born to you in the land of Egypt before I came to you in Egypt, are mine, Ephraim and Manasseh shall be mine, as Reuben and Simeon are" (Genesis 48:5).

Ephraim became a chosen son, thoroughly grafted into Israel, though he was the son of a mixed marriage. In Isaiah 56:6–8, we read a very revealing passage of Scripture:

"Also the foreigners who join themselves to the LORD, to minister to Him, and to love the name of the LORD, to be His servants, every one of them who keeps from profaning the Sabbath, and holds fast my covenant; even those I will bring to My holy mountain and make them joyful in My house of prayer ... The LORD God who gathers the dispersed of Israel, declares, 'Yet others I will gather to them to those already gathered.'"

The gathering of others to the dispersed of Israel already started with Ephraim, a child of a mixed marriage with a very big promise. The LORD will have a crop of children from the nations, and Ephraim is the chosen one to bring this crop in. This "crop" culminates in Romans 11:25 as we say that "the fullness of the Gentiles" will come in through the gospel and then all of Israel will be saved as it is written. So, let's find out what is written. Let's follow the word "Ephraim" in the Scriptures and find out what he became.

We know that upon the conquering of the land of Canaan by Joshua and the twelve tribes, Ephraim settled to the north of Judah and Jerusalem in the hill country. That area is today between Bethel and Samaria. It even spreads to the Jezreel Valley because they became so many people (Joshua 17:14–17). The word "Ephraim" in Hebrew means "the fruitful one," in other words, the "one that multiplies abundantly."

In 1 Kings 12:25–33 we see the rise of a king by the name of Jeroboam Ben Nebath. This king was not from the tribe of

Judah; he was an Ephramite. He ruled over the ten northern tribes of Israel after the split that took place in Israel upon the death of King Solomon. A prophet by the name of Ahia the Shilonite prophesied of this split to Jeroboam. He told him that God was granting Jeroboam ten of the tribes, although he was not of the lineage of King David, the kingly line .

From that very moment, there was a broken brotherhood between the tribe of Judah, who by then had merged with Benjamin and Levi, and the rest of the northern tribes ruled by Jeroboam. In Zechariah 11:14 we read of this painful "divorce" in Israel:

"Then I cut my second staff, Union, in pieces, to break the brotherhood between Judah and Israel."

The House of Judah was the kingdom of the South with Jerusalem as its capital, and the House of Israel was the kingdom of the North with Samaria in the country of Ephraim as its capital. Later on, the Northern kingdom was also called Ephraim. The brotherhood was "broken to pieces," which means that no human hands could put them together again.

Jeroboam, from the tribe of Ephraim started ruling over the ten tribes. He caused them to go into great idolatry. He wanted to prevent them from going to worship at the Temple in Jerusalem and from regaining their identity as brothers of the tribe of Judah as children of the LORD. So, he built golden calves in Bethel and in Dan and divorced Israel from having any contact with Judah. He also expelled all the Levites from their midst and raised up a false priesthood system. It was to this scene that the prophet Elijah arrives and challenges all the prophets of Baal on Mount Carmel: Elijah was calling Ephraim to go back to the Law of the LORD. That included the Temple Worship in Jerusalem .

Finally, the LORD was very angry with the House of Israel, or Ephraim. So that brings a prophet by the name of Hosea. The name of this prophet is very revealing as well. It means "save us," as in Hosanna. Hosea married a prostitute and had two children by her, a boy by the name of Lo Ammi, which means "not My people," and a girl by the name of Lo Ruhamah, which means "no compassion." "... for I will no longer have compassion on the house of Israel that I should ever forgive them. But I will have compassion on the House of Judah ..." (Hosea 1:6–7).

From that very moment, a process started, a process of total rejection of the House of Israel, or Ephraim. "Ephraim is oppressed, crushed in judgment, because he was determined to follow man's command" (Hosea 5:11). "When I would heal Israel, the iniquity of Ephraim is uncovered, and the evil deeds of Samaria, for they deal falsely ..." (Hosea 7:1). "Ephraim is stricken, their root is dried up, they will bear no fruit ... My God will cast them away because they have not listened to Him; and they will be wanderers among the nations" (Hosea 9:16–17).

Ephraim, "the fruitful one," is cursed to bear no more fruit and to mix with the nations, "So the LORD was angry with Israel, and he removed them from His sight; none was left except the tribe of Judah" (2 Kings 17:18).

The Assyrians had their special ways with the people they conquered. They used to separate them and scatter them among their empire. In that way, a people that was conquered could never again rise against the Assyrian empire, as their national unity was broken. This they did in conquering Ephraim. At the same time, they brought pagans from the Assyrian empire to settle in Samaria, the capital of Ephraim or the Northern Kingdom of Israel. From that time, the 8th Century BC, Ephraim was lost along with all the ten tribes. It sounds like a great defeat and a very sad ending to the story but, in the midst of all this distress, the God of Israel was devising His plan. He was making sure that Ephraim would fulfill his call as the "fullness of the nations." He said in Hosea 1:11 a cryptic thing, "Great will be the day of Jezreel," which can be translated, Great shall be the day of the LORD's sowing.

And if the LORD has sown He shall surely reap. He sowed Ephraim into the nations and He has a plan for how to reap Ephraim as the fullness of the nations.

CHAPTER SIX

"Ruhamah"

"Yet the number of the sons of Israel will be like the sand of the sea, which cannot be measured or numbered; and it will come about that, in the place where it is said to them, 'You are not My people' it will be said to them, 'You are the sons of the living God.'"

—HOSEA 1:10

R UHAMAH MEANS: "THE ONE who has received compassion." In this chapter I will call the church Ruhamah.

The God of Israel is never in confusion and yet it seems to be that in the book of Hosea He was contradicting Himself. On the one hand, He had cut off the ten northern tribes (or Ephraim) from being His people to the point where He said that He would never forgive them. And, on the other hand, He stated, "I will also have compassion on her ..." (Hosea 2:23). So, what was He saying?

I believe that He was saying, "I have cut you off from being children of the covenant and, in that sense, you will not be Israel any longer and you cannot claim your rights as children of Abraham. You are totally cut off. Yet, when you mix with the nations, you will forget who you are, and you will become uncircumcised Gentiles. And as uncircumcised Gentiles I will have compassion over you!"

The children of Israel are mixed with all the nations, to the point that today in every tribe and nation, there is Israeli blood mixed with the Gentiles. Ephraim who has multiplied abundantly has become thoroughly mixed with the nations. In his ignorance of God, he hears the call of the LORD through the Cross. And when he comes in as a Gentile through the Blood of the New Covenant, God says to him, "Now I call you, My people, now you are sons of the living God." It is indeed an amazing plan, but then, we serve an amazing God.

In Romans 9:24–26, Paul confirms this as he quotes from Hosea, "... even us, whom He also called not from among Jews only, but also from among Gentiles, as He says also in Hosea, I will call those who were not 'My People', My people, and her who was not beloved, 'Beloved'. And it shall be that in the place where it was said to them, 'You are not My people', there they shall be called sons of the living God." In other words, Paul is saying, "You are Ephraim who was mixed with the nations, and now as Gentiles, God has compassion over you and He calls you My people again!"

Can you imagine the wound of rejection that Ephraim carried to the nations? First, he was disconnected from his brothers, Judah and Levi. A totally broken brotherhood had surely left its mark of rejection. Then, through the sin of Jeroboam that caused all of Israel to go into idolatry, there is also a divorce from the LORD and from Temple worship. Finally, Ephraim, the Northern kingdom, is expelled from his land and rejection comes to its climax!

Let us review this for a moment. The wound of rejection in Ephraim is so deep that it covers every area of their lives:

1. Separation from God and Jerusalem
2. Separation from Judah their brothers
3. Separation from the land of Israel and their inheritance

From my limited understanding of the problem of rejection, it seems to me that if rejection is untreated it can never get better. It actually worsens with time, creating a stony heart, a heart that is protected by many layers of hardness. Generally, bitterness arises.

Because of an unfulfilled longing to be together with our lost relatives, we actually develop bitterness against them, and deep within our hearts we start blaming them as the cause of our rejection.

The persecution of Christians against Jews in the nations has had all the signs of this process. Every time Jews have been persecuted by Christians, it's "because the Jews are to blame for all of our problems."

The Gentiles who have come into the Kingdom through the cross still carry with them in their bloodline "the rejection of Ephraim." So, the very presence of the Jews causes those wounds of rejection to open up and to start a reaction of anti-Semitism. This vicious circle can never be defeated until we repent from blaming our brothers for our misfortunes and, through this, come to the fullness of the love of the Father, that though He rejected the ten tribes, yet He has had compassion. He has brought them in as the fullness of the Gentiles, as Ruhamah, as the one who has received compassion.

This repentance is a very deep process of cleansing. It will take us into our family line, all the way back to the land of Ephraim and to Samaria, and even as far as the sin of Jeroboam.

That is why I call the sin of Constantine of divorcing the church from its Jewish roots in the 4th Century, the sin of Jeroboam in the church. This divorce has caused the wound of rejection and alienation and estrangement to deepen in the church. Only repentance from anti-Semitism, and reconnection with our Roots can heal that wound.

Another root problem that a large portion of Christians have which has caused a tremendous amount of cruelty and anti-Semitism, is jealousy. Jealousy is an outcome of rejection,

"Jealousy is as cruel as the grave; the coals thereof are coals of fire which hath a most vehement flame" (Song of Songs 8:6, KJV). The ovens of Auschwitz, Bergen-Belsen and Treblinka during the Nazi regime where so many of my people were exterminated had the smell of jealousy! "Jealousy enrages a man, and he will not spare in the day of vengeance" (Proverbs 6:34); "And He will lift up a standard for the nations and will assemble the banished ones of Israel. And will gather the dispersed of Judah from the four comers of the earth. Then the jealousy of Ephraim will depart, and those who harass Judah will be cut off; Ephraim will not be jealous of Judah ..." (Isaiah 11:12,13).

This is the time that God is gathering the dispersed ones of Judah. From all over the world the Jewish people are being brought to their homeland, Israel. The outcome of this ingathering is that, finally, Ephraim will not be jealous anymore.

Since Ephraim became "the fullness of the Gentiles," this harmful jealousy has affected many Christians. I have personally experienced the jealousy of Ephraim many times, especially from Christians who have previously accepted me and opened their hearts to my ministry as a Messianic Jew. It's a vicious circle: they accept me and proclaim their great love for Israel and for the Jewish people, they love the anointing and the prophetic ministry, we become friends, then, all of a sudden, jealousy starts rising to the surface. Without understanding why, they start lashing out against me and the ministry in subtle ways. Then the spirit manifesting from these same brothers and sisters seeks to kill, quench and destroy the anointing in me! Sometimes it is under the guise of "wisdom," "protection," "for my own good," "for the good of the people" and so on. My heart then starts aching deeply and I recognize that I am again in the presence of the Jealousy of Ephraim.

Many times, during our Back to the Roots seminars, as people are repenting, someone will approach me and confess to me that they have been jealous of me and they do not know why. The same thing happens in the story of *The Prodigal Son*. As the father receives him back from being lost, with open arms and a great celebration, the other son who stayed home all the time becomes jealous and refuses to partake of the celebration. The father comforts him by saying, "... All that is mine is yours" (Luke 15:11-32).

One of the main reasons for this age-old jealousy is that Judah is the kingly tribe. From the tribe of Judah came King David ... from that tribe came King Yeshua (Jesus)!

What is the remedy for jealousy? To my understanding the only remedy is: Repentance.

1. Recognizing the problem
2. Confessing it out loud before the LORD and before someone else, preferably a Jew
3. Repenting and renouncing it as sin
4. Allowing humility to come in and any selfish desires to die
5. Asking God to help you understand the full extent of the love of the Father for you.

With all of these, humility is the key. It is connected with taking an active part in the natural restoration of the Jewish people to their land, "Thus says the LORD God, 'Behold I will lift up My hand to the nations and set up My standards to the peoples; and they will bring your sons in their bosom and your daughters will be carried on their shoulders. And kings will be your guardians, and their princesses your nurses. They will bow down to you with their faces to the earth and lick the dust of your feet; and you will know that I am the LORD'" (Isaiah 49:22–23). Who could be these humble kings and queens? There is no doubt in my mind that those are the sons of God, the real Christians!

Once, in the midst of one of our prophetic conferences, as the Holy Spirit took over, we were dancing and worshiping the LORD, and the spirit of repentance fell on all of us. There we were on the floor weeping. Many people were weeping for the Jews. A prophetess friend of ours started kissing my feet and my husband's feet. As she was doing that and washing our feet with her tears, I was weeping as well. I asked her, "Did you know the Scripture from Isaiah 49, about kings and queens bowing down before the Jews at the time of their restoration?" She said, "I have never read that verse before. The Holy Spirit showed me to do this!" This, of course, was a prophetic conference, where the Holy Spirit was allowed the freedom to minister in a prophetic manner. And He led her to literally do the word!

We must proclaim a holy war against this age-old destructive jealousy. "Wrath is fierce and anger is a flood, but who can stand before jealousy?" (Proverbs 27:4) Repentance and humility are the keys!

We also need to remember that, although Jeroboam caused the Israelites to sin, the LORD punished them all. He held them all accountable. In the same way, though Constantine made the divorce from the Jewish roots official, we, as believers, are all accountable. We, like Daniel in Babylon (Daniel 9:3–20), need to have collective accountability and to repent personally.

There is a mixture of paganism in the church today that the LORD will intensely cleanse, as we approach the end of this era. For example, the pagan rites that accompany the celebration of Easter ... the looking for eggs, the bunny rabbits ... these are all leftovers from pagan fertility rites. They accompanied the orgies and slaughter of the babies who were conceived after these orgies. Then, eggs were dipped in their blood. Rabbits are very prolific animals, so they are a symbol of fertility. Even the name Easter is derived from the goddess of fertility, Ishtar. Why would we keep calling our celebrations of Messiah by pagan names? Or use pagan rites? The LORD God is holy, and we are a holy people set apart and separated from the ways of this world.

There are a lot more examples. We need to allow a holy cleansing and conviction to happen to us. Every denomination of Christianity has traditions that are unholy. We have to be humble enough to present all of our traditions before the LORD and let Him reveal to us what is holy and what is totally unbiblical.

Going back to the roots is an answer to the mixture of paganism in the church. We need to start taking God's Word and Law literally, as revealed to us by His Holy Spirit. The LORD is calling us to humble ourselves and to let Him check our hearts and our ways if they be pleasing unto Him. A holy, healthy fear of God and of His Word will be returned to us, as we let ourselves be grafted back into the original roots of the church.

History tends to repeat itself. A new wave of persecution against the Jews is about to arise. In fact, all the nations are about to come against Jerusalem, "For I will gather all the nations against Jerusalem to battle, and the city will be captured, the houses plundered, the women ravished, and half of the city exiled, but the rest of the people will not be cut off from the city. Then the LORD will go forth and fight against those nations, as when He fights in the day of battle" (Zechariah 14:2–3).

Where will the Christians be in this battle? Will they stand alongside their brothers this time and support them, or will they, too, blame them again for all the evil in the world?

Healing from the rejection of Ephraim is the key. A healed and cleansed church, a Ruhamah church is also about to arise. When it arises, filled with love for Israel and for their Jewish brothers, the world will know that the Father sent the Son!

A Prayer of Repentance and Healing

Please pray this prayer in order to start a deep healing from rejection:

Dear Father in heaven, thank You for having compassion over me, a Gentile who was totally cut off from the promises of Israel. Thank You for bringing me near through the precious blood of the New Covenant. Please forgive me for not extending the same compassion also to my Jewish brothers – and even to those who are still in unbelief. I realize that You gave them up for a season so that I might be saved. Please help me realize the full extent of Your compassion. I accept Your love, and fully renounce all rejection, jealousy, and bitterness in my life. I also renounce any idolatrous and pagan traditions that I may have. I place all of my religious traditions before You and I ask You to reveal to me the ones that do not please You. I open myself up so that You can lead me through a process of repentance and healing. I thank you, LORD, that I am Your Ruhamah. Help me to be Ruhamah to everyone in my path and especially to my people, the Jews. In the name of Yeshua (Jesus), I pray. Amen.

CHAPTER SEVEN

Ruhamah in Travail

"And I will betroth you to Me forever; yes, I will betroth you
to Me in faithfulness, in loving kindness and in compassion."

—HOSEA 2:19

I N THE PREVIOUS CHAPTER I called the church "Ruhamah," the one who has received compassion. In this chapter I would like to go deeper into our "wedding preparations" as the Bride of Messiah, to the King of the Universe and the role that compassion will play in this prophetic preparation. In Matthew 9:36 (KJV) we read, "But when he saw the multitudes, he was moved with compassion on them, because they were scattered abroad, as sheep having no shepherd." Yeshua's motivation for ministry was mainly compassion.

Today the Jewish people are like sheep with no shepherd, especially the young generation and the soldiers. They are looking for something to fill them. They need to experience a move of compassion coming from the church. In Mark 1:41 we read, "And moved with compassion, He stretched out His hand, and touched him and said to him, 'I am willing; be cleansed.'" Here we see that the LORD cleanses people, not because He is upset with them, but because He is moved with compassion.

One of the most lacking components in the church is compassion. Everywhere we go in the world, we meet wounded sheep,

sheep that have experienced no compassion from their leaders or from their peers.

However, having no compassion is like denying the faith because the name of the "cut off branches" was *lo ruhamah* (Hosea 1), which means, "no compassion." That is the name of Ephraim who became "the fullness of the Gentiles," as we have seen in previous chapters.

So, what is compassion? Compassion in Hebrew is rahamim. From this word, we derive the word *ruhamah*, or the "one who has received compassion." *Rahamim* also means "a multitude of wombs" (as the womb of a pregnant woman). It implies birthing and travailing, children, motherhood, tender loving care, instruction, protection and a generous dose of forgiveness. It also implies total acceptance and patience for the processes of growth. Rahamim is a consummation of the total, unconditional, unselfish, patient, confident love of a mother who is willing to give up her life in order to bring a baby forth, no matter what the cost, or the pain or the suffering. The mother who is willing to give of her time and comfort in order to provide tender, nurturing, loving care and correction for this baby to grow up healthy in spirit, soul and body so that he can confidently fulfill his call in life.

That is how Yeshua walked. That is what moved Him. That is how He has treated us. And that is how He expects us to treat others.

This call to be Ruhamah to a lost and dying world is our major call. This call to be Ruhamah to our fellow Christians is our major call. This is the call on the leadership of the body of the Lord today. Be Ruhamah to My sheep!

So many times I hear unkind and condemning remarks from leaders about the people under their care. So many times I need to check my own heart and my own tongue when I speak about people. So many times we are unwilling to give ourselves up for someone else to grow. So often we forget our name and our calling as Ruhamah. We shut our wombs of compassion because of selfishness and self-pity.

Mothers often get hurt when they care for their children. Sometimes the children are ungrateful or disappointing in their development. It takes God's love and God's grace to keep our bowels of mercy open, but we do not have any other choice... we are called Ruhamah.

Even as I am writing this book, the LORD is working within my heart about what I'm writing. Last night He gave me a dream to illustrate the point of this chapter.

The Dream

I was very busy, standing at a bus stop, talking on my cellular phone. I was making an important call to the hospital, as I thought that my father was in the hospital.

At the same bus station was a very distressed woman with a baby in a carriage. She said to me, "Please make a phone call for me on your cellular phone. I'll pay you for the expenses. I need to communicate with my home as this bus is taking too long and the baby is sick."

My response was very cold and detached and self-important. "I will help you later. First, I have to make my call which is more important to me."

As I was trying to dial the number of the hospital, my brand-new camera that I was holding in my hands fell to the ground and rolled under some cars. I had to stop my phone call, trying desperately to search for the camera. But it was hidden from my sight. I could not recover it.

I woke up from this dream very distressed, asking God what He was trying to tell me. The interpretation came right away: I failed to have compassion for a person in need, putting my important matters first, thinking that what I was doing was more important than helping her. My camera represented prophetic revelation. The LORD was communicating with me that if I have no compassion, I will lose all prophetic revelation!

I immediately repented before God and, as I finished doing so, He gave me this chapter that I am writing. I believe this is the Word of the LORD for the church and especially for prophetically anointed ministries: without a selfless compassion we will lose our sight.

Compassion is the antidote to pride and arrogance.

The church is called to be a priest and a prophet in the world. Without compassion, our priestly and prophetic ministry is perverted. We are called to be Ruhamah to Judah, to the Jewish people; to extend compassion to her who has had no compassion, "Comfort, O comfort My people, says your God. Speak kindly to Jerusalem; and call out to her, that her warfare has ended, that her iniquity has been removed, that she has received of the LORD's hand double for all her sins" (Isaiah 40:1–2).

A German lady in America told us of a dramatic experience she had with the LORD. She was lying next to a swimming pool and suddenly a vein burst in her head (also called an aneurysm). She was rushed to the hospital clinically dead.

Meanwhile she found herself walking in heaven with the LORD. He was showing her a few rooms. Then He took her to a certain room where she saw a very handsome and self-assured man coming towards Jesus. The LORD addressed him and said, "And what have you done for My people?"

To that, the man full of pride and self-satisfaction replied, "O LORD I have cast out demons in your name, I have healed the sick in your name, I have opened blind eyes in your name" ... and on and on he went.

The LORD, very serious and insistent, asked him again, "Yes, but what have you done for My people?"

"O LORD, I told you. I raised the dead, opened deaf ears..."

The LORD said, "Have you heard of the Scripture, 'Comfort, O comfort My people'?"

"Of course, I have, LORD, that is my favorite Scripture for the church."

To which the LORD replied in a stern voice, "Depart from Me into outer darkness, I never knew you!"

Then He turned to the German woman and said, "Go back and tell the church to repent for not extending mercy and compassion to My people, the Jews."

This lady came back to the living and brought with her this message.

Dear Ruhamah, we are the church of the LORD. He is preparing our wedding garment. But neither the Bride, nor the Wedding will be ready until we lay our lives down for the LORD's people, Israel. They have been persecuted and slandered in the name of Jesus. Now the LORD is extending an invitation which is also a Commandment, "Comfort my people, travail for them to come forth, be like Ruth was to Naomi, and stick to them even in their unbelief. Be like a mother to them. They need your love and commitment in order to start believing in the goodness of the LORD. Be Ruhamah to them and extend the same compassion that has been extended to you."

As you do that, there is a very special promise for you, "Be joyful with Jerusalem and rejoice for her, all you who love her;

be exceedingly glad with her, all you who mourn over her, that you may nurse and be satisfied with her comforting breasts ..." (Isaiah 66:10–11).

As we extend comfort and mercy to Jerusalem and to our Jewish brothers, Jerusalem will, in time, turn and be our comfort. For as we travail for Israel to come forth, she will become Ruhamah, "the one who has received compassion," just as the church is now Ruhamah. Then they will be one Bride before the LORD, one nation, one people, with one God.

A Prayer of Response

Please pray this prayer with me in order to allow God to deal with our lack of compassion!

Dear Father in heaven, I come before You, bowing down before Your feet, laying down all of my gifts and anointings, ministries and callings. Father, I ask You to cleanse me of my lack of compassion, pride, arrogance, selfishness, and self-importance. I renounce all of that in the name of Yeshua, and I pray that You eradicate it from my soul and spirit. Father, help me to walk in full compassion, in the fullness of what Ruhamah means. LORD, use me as a vessel of comfort and compassion in the church, to the lost and especially to Your Jewish people. Amen.

CHAPTER EIGHT

Grafted In

"Listen to me, you who pursue righteousness, who seek the LORD: Look to the rock from which you were hewn, and to the quarry from which you were dug. Look to Abraham your father, and to Sarah who gave birth to you in pain; When he was one, I called him, then I blessed him and multiplied him."

—ISAIAH 51:1–2

N OW WE CAN LOOK back to our roots, to our ori-
gins. The reason why we are children of God today
is only because of one man, that man is Abraham.
God promised Abraham that his seed would be as the stars in
heaven and as the sand on the seashore that cannot be counted.
He told him that this promise and this covenant would be
extended to his son, Isaac. Later on, He appeared to Jacob,
confirming the covenant (Genesis 22:16–17; 26:4; 28:14).

In Hebrew, the word for seed is *zerah*. Zerah can only be natural, like the male sperm or the seed of a plant.

So, when the LORD sowed Ephraim among the nations, He
sowed the natural seed of Abraham that multiplied and became
"the fullness of the Gentiles."

In that sense, the LORD was fulfilling His promise to Abraham
that his zerah, his seed, would become as "the stars in heaven."
God does not waste the seed of Abraham. He is a good farmer.
He always sows for and expects a plentiful crop!

In Romans 11:17 it says, "But if some of the (natural) branches
were broken off, and you being a wild olive tree, were grafted in
among them and became partaker with them of the rich root of

the olive tree, do not be arrogant towards the branches." What is a wild olive tree? And what is the difference between a wild olive tree and a cultivated olive tree?

First of all, we need to know olive trees live for a long, long time. There are some ancient olive trees in Israel today that could have been there even in Yeshua's time.

Secondly, we need to know olive trees produce a fruit, the olive. This fruit contains a high content of oil. Olive oil was used in the Temple worship. It was used by the prophets when they anointed the kings of Israel. And it was used by the shepherds to rub into the wounds of their sheep.

Thirdly, the way "wild" olive trees are produced is when branches of a cultivated olive tree are broken off and neglected and grow by themselves. When a wild olive grows like this, it normally tends to spread very rapidly and have a lot of very thin fruit, fruit without much oil.

When the ten tribes of Israel multiplied throughout the nations, they became uncultivated, unattended wild olive trees. But through the message of the Cross, they become grafted into the cultivated olive tree. That tree is Israel. Being grafted into the cultivated olive tree is being grafted into the nation of Israel. "Therefore remember, that formerly you, the Gentiles in the flesh, who are called 'Uncircumcision' by the so called 'Circumcision' which is performed in the flesh by human hands – remember that you were at that time separate from Christ, excluded from the commonwealth of Israel and strangers to the covenant of promise, having no hope and without God in the world. But now in Christ Jesus you who formerly were far off have been brought near by the blood of Christ" (Ephesians 2:11–13). Being "grafted in" means that you now belong to the commonwealth of Israel. Not that you have replaced Israel, but you have actually rejoined Israel.

Now we can understand Romans 11:11. "I say then, they did not stumble so as to fall, did they? May it never be! But by their transgression salvation has come to the Gentiles to make them jealous." God is wanting to use the church to make the Jews jealous and eager to have their God back! But a church which is divorced from its roots and alienated from the commonwealth of Israel and from the Torah, can never make a Jew jealous. A church which celebrates pagan feasts and rejects the holy feasts of the LORD, which worships a Gentile Jesus, instead of the Jewish Messiah who He is, can never fulfill its call to cause the Jews to be jealous.

One of the major strongholds that developed after the divorce from our roots is that Yeshua became "Gentilized." We cannot relate to Him as a Jew anymore. But being grafted in means that we accept both the Jewish Messiah and His people, who are actually our own people.

In the book of Revelation, Yeshua (Jesus) is called "the Lion of the Tribe of Judah" (Revelation 5:5). He is also called our Mediator, "the man Jesus the Messiah" (I Timothy 2:5). He has the marks of the nails in His hands; don't you think He also has the marks of circumcision in His body (Luke 2:21)? Yeshua (Jesus) rose from the dead as a man with a glorified body. So, His identity remains Jewish all the way through the book of Revelation. He is still the "Son of David" and the Son of David is a Jew (Matthew 1:1).

The LORD has chosen a Jew to rule for all eternity. Therefore, His bride, as depicted in Revelation 21, is an Israeli bride. The gates are the twelve tribes of Israel. The foundation stones are the twelve Jewish apostles of the Lamb. The Jewish Messiah is the fulfillment of the promise to Abraham! As we are "grafted in" through Him into His people, we become one with a unity that is not of this world.

When Yeshua prayed in John 17:22–23 that we may all be one, He was talking to the Jews. All the believers were Jews at that time. He was saying that others would come in through their message. He was actually saying: When they come in, accept them as part of the "Commonwealth of Israel." Become one with them as your own "flesh and blood" (Ephesians 2:12).

Many Jews are about to join the body. They cannot join a Gentilized church. Many of them will have a prophetic word of restoration back to the roots.

The LORD is about to make Jerusalem His throne, as depicted in Jeremiah 3:17. He will come back to Jerusalem for His thousand-year reign (Revelation 20:4). Now He is preparing His city, His Jewish people and His church. Many things will change as the LORD restores all of the truth that has been stolen from the church, as He heals the outcome of this age-old divorce from our roots.

There is a lot of talk about unity in the body of Messiah. We all want to break dividing walls and become one. That unity can only be attained if we go back to our roots to become one within the olive tree, and not invent another religious system. I do not mean we have to become religious Jews and practice Rabbinical Judaism. What I mean is that we have to allow the Law to be written on our hearts and be reconnected to our biblical roots: Jeremiah 31:31–33, "Behold, days are coming," declares the LORD, "when I will make a New Covenant with the House of Israel and with the House of Judah, not like the covenant which I made with their fathers in the day I took them by the hand to bring them out of the land of Egypt, My covenant which they broke, although I was a husband to them," declares the LORD. "But this is the covenant which I will make with the House of Israel after those days," declares the LORD, "I will put My Law within them, and on their hearts, I will write it; and I will be their God, and they shall be My people."

Notice this New Covenant is to be made with the two Houses, or the two sides of the kingdom of Israel – the House of Israel, which represents Ephraim and the "fullness of the Gentiles," and with the House of Judah, which represents the Jewish people of today.

Now we can understand what is written in Ezekiel 37:15–17: The Word of the LORD came again to me saying, "And you son of man, take for yourself one stick and write on it, 'For Judah and for the sons of Israel, his companions'; then take another stick and write on it, 'For Joseph, the stick of Ephraim and all the house of Israel his companions'. Then join them for yourself one to another into one stick, that they may become one in your hand."

There is a powerful unity coming. The LORD is about to unite the church and Judah, so that together they become the bride of Christ. The "fullness of the Gentiles" is coming in great numbers. And then, all of Israel is going to be saved, just as it is written.

A Concluding Prayer

Dear heavenly Father, I thank You that You are an awesome God, One who keeps covenant and shows mercy even unto a thousand generations. Thank You that You never forgot Your covenant with Abraham, Isaac and Jacob. Thank You that as I am re-grafted into Israel and I belong to the "commonwealth of Israel." the people of Israel are my people and I love them. I accept You, Yeshua, as my Jewish Messiah. Thank You that You are "the Lion of the Tribe of Judah." I am now a partaker of the rich root of the olive tree and I stand in agreement with Your Word that all of Israel will be saved. I ask You to use me to make my Jewish brothers jealous of my walk with You, so that they will come back to You. Please teach me practical ways on how to extend mercy and compassion to the Jewish people so that they may be called Ruhamah as well. In Yeshua's name, I pray. Amen.

Epilogue

"For the Law, since it has only a shadow of the good things to come and not the very form of things, can never by the same sacrifices year by year, which they offer continually, make perfect those who draw near... Then I said, 'Behold, I have come to do Thy will, O God'... then He said 'Behold, I have come to do Thy will'... He takes away the first in order to establish the second.... 'This is the covenant that I will make with them after those days' says the LORD: 'I will put My Laws upon their heart, and upon their mind I will write them'... Since therefore, brethren, we have confidence to enter the holy place by the blood of Jesus (Yeshua).... let us consider how to stimulate one another to love and good deeds... For if we go on sinning willfully after receiving the knowledge of the truth, there no longer remains a sacrifice for sins.

—HEBREWS 10:1,7,9,16,19,24,26

D EAR READER, I HOPE the LORD has spoken to you about this subject. I am fully aware that there is more to say about this important subject, especially about the Torah. The Torah is the shadow of the real thing. The Bible has a lot to say about shadows. It was Peter's shadow that healed the sick (Acts 5:15). In Psalms 91:1, it says, "He who dwells in the shelter of the Most High will abide in the shadow of the Almighty." In John 15:7, it is written, "If you abide in Me and My Words abide in you, ask whatever you wish, and it shall be done for you." The Torah is the shadow of Yeshua and Yeshua is the Torah, "the Word made flesh" (John 1:1,14). Is the shadow of the Messiah abolished? Is there any healing in His shadow? When we accept His blood, we start living in Him and He becomes our shelter. We become one with Him. Therefore, we share the same shadow – the same Torah.

When we accept His blood sacrifice, it is not in order to continue to go our own way. It is in order to have His Laws and His instructions written on our hearts. The Ten Commandments are eternal, and so is every word that has ever proceeded out of His mouth. As it is written in James 1:17, He has no shadow of turning in Him. Every jot and tittle from His Torah have an important meaning. The dietary Laws protect us from sickness and impurity. The Shabbat protects us from exhaustion and chronic fatigue syndrome. The moral Laws protect us from social destruction. Each instruction in the Torah also has a prophetic meaning that can enable us to know our Messiah more intimately. Every one of the biblical holidays reveals the Messiah and different aspects of the gospel. The Holy Spirit's job is to interpret the Torah to us. Let us now walk in the Spirit and abide in the shadow of the Almighty.

A new reformation is knocking at the doors of the church. Some of us will tend to resist it. My prayer is that this book will be a tool in God's hand to facilitate our yielding to this new move of restoration back to our roots. Now that you know you are "grafted in," you know that you are a very important part in this restoration.

You probably have many questions about many passages of Scripture coming to your mind. "So what about Galatians and Romans and Acts?" I can only encourage you to follow the leading of your questions and inquire of the Holy Spirit and the Word. I suggest that as you read the New Testament, now with different eyes, that you start noticing a few things:

- Who is a specific letter written to?
- What is the background to the writing of a specific letter?
- What is the issue they were dealing with? (For example, in the book of Galatians, Paul was dealing with some people who were trying to convince the believers that the only way to get saved was through physical circumcision rather than the circumcision of the heart).

Be careful of some Bible versions when they introduce a word in italics. This means that word is not in the original manuscript and it has been interpreted by the writer of that particular version.

And please do not forget that no one is infallible and that each one of us has a "piece of the puzzle" of the all-encompassing revelation of God and His marvelous Word. I believe that it is essential to maintain a humble, searching heart at all times since the revelation of God is progressive.

Prayer for Forgiveness

Please pray this prayer with me, in order to receive forgiveness for your sins:

God of Abraham, Isaac and Jacob, I come before Your Throne in humility to ask You to forgive me of all of my sins (list your sins if you can). I accept the blood atonement on the Cross, of Your Son and my Jewish Messiah, Yeshua (Jesus). Yeshua, I believe that You are the Way, the Truth and the Life. I believe that You paid for all my sins so that I can be reconciled to my heavenly Father, the God of Israel. I believe that You rose from the dead and that You are alive. I accept You as my LORD, my Messiah and Savior. Please fill me with Your Holy Spirit so that I may learn to walk in Your ways. And lead me to a fellowship of believers, so that I can grow in my faith. Thank you for Eternal life. In Yeshua's name, I pray. Amen.

If you have prayed this prayer for the first time, congratulations! You have just taken the most important step in your life. Please make sure you get a full Bible, which includes the Tanakh and the New Testament (Old and New Testament).

If you are a Jew, welcome back! The church accepts you with open arms. We ask your forgiveness for all the atrocities we have committed against you and your people. Please start reading the New Testament from the beginning as a personal love letter from God to you. Ask the Holy Spirit to illuminate your reading.

If you are a Gentile, welcome to the Commonwealth of Israel! We accept you with open arms. Please start reading the entire bible from today, asking the Holy Spirit to talk to you.

Bibliography

» *The Bible.* Authorized King James Version, Oxford UP, 1998.

» *The Bible.* New American Standard Bible, The Lockman Foundation, 1977

» *The Bible*, Tree of Life Version, Copyright © 2014 - Messianic Jewish Family Bible Society

» Percival, Dr. Henry R. *The Nicean and post Nicean Fathers.* Vol. XIV Grand Rapids: Erdmans. 1979, pp. 54-55.

» Wilson, Marvin R. *Our Father Abraham: Jewish Roots of the Christian Faith.* Grand Rapids and Dayton:Wm. B. Eerdmans Publishing Company and Center for Judaic-Christian Studies, 1989.

» Luther, Martin. *Ninety-five Theses on the Power and Efficacy of Indulgences*, 1517

» Luther, Martin. *On the Jews and their Lies. First English Translation.* Los Angeles. Christian Nationalist Crusade, 1948.

Other Books by Archbishop Dr. Dominiquae Bierman

Order now online: www.ZionsGospel.com

The MAP Revolution (Free E-Book)
Exposing Theologies that Obstruct the Bride

The Identity Theft
The Return of the 1st Century Messiah

Grafted In
The Return to Greatness

Sheep Nations
It's Time to Take the Nations!

Restoring the Glory: The Original Way
The Ancient Paths Rediscovered

Stormy Weather
Judgment Has Already Begun, Revival is
Knocking at the Door

Yeshua is the Name
The Important Restoration of the Original
Hebrew Name of the Messiah

The Bible Cure for Africa and the Nations
The Key to the Restoration of All Africa

The Key of Abraham
The Blessing or the Curse?

Yes!
The Dramatic Salvation of Archbishop Dr. Dominiquae Bierman

Eradicating the Cancer of Religion
Hint: All People Have It

Restoration of Holy Giving
Releasing the True 1,000 Fold Blessing

Vision Negev
The Awesome Restoration of the Sephardic Jews

Defeating Depression
This Book is a Kiss from Heaven

From Sickology to a Healthy Logic
The Product of 18 Years Walking Through Psychiatric Hospitals

ATG: Addicts Turning to God
The Biblical Way to Handle Addicts and Addictions

The Woman Factor by Rabbi Baruch Bierman
Freedom From Womanphobia

Let's Get Healthy, Saints!
The Biblical Guide to Health

The Revival of the Third Day (Free E-Book)
The Return to Yeshua the Jewish Messiah

Tribute to the Jew in You Music Book
Notes for the Tribute to the Jew in You Music Album

Also Available

Music Albums
www.ZionsGospel.com
The Key of Abraham

Abba Shebashamayim
Uru
Retorno
Tribute to the Jew in You
Tribute to the Jew in You Instrumental

Get Equipped & Partner with Us

Global Revival MAP (GRM) Israeli Bible School
Take the most life-changing video Bible school online that
focuses on restoring the gospel of the 1st century.
For more information or to order, please contact us:
www.grmbibleschool.com | grm@dominiquaebierman.com

United Nations for Israel Movement
We invite you to join us as a member and partner with $25
a month, which supports the advancing of this End time
vision that will bring true unity to the body of the Messiah.
We will see the One New Man form, witness the restoration of
Israel, and take part in the birthing of Sheep Nations. Today is
an exciting time to be serving Him!
www.unitednationsforisrael.org
info@unitednationsforisrael.org

Global Re-Education Initiative Against Anti-Semitism (GRI)
Discover the Jewishness of Jesus and defeat Christian
anti-Semitism with this online video course to see revival
in your nation!
www.against-antisemitism.com
info@against-antisemitism.com

Join Our Annual Israel Tours
Travel through the Holy Land and watch the Hebrew
Holy Scriptures come alive.
www.kad-esh.org/tours-and-events/

To Send Offerings to Support our Work
Your help keeps this mission of restoration going far and wide.
www.kad-esh.org/donations

Contact us

Archbishop Dr. Dominiquae & Rabbi Baruch Bierman
Kad-Esh MAP Ministries | www.kad-esh.org | info@kad-esh.org
United Nations for Israel | www.unitednationsforisrael.org
info@unitednationsforisrael.org

Resources

Zion's Gospel Press | www.zionsgospel.com
shalom@zionsgospel.com | +1-972-301-7087
52 Tuscan Way, Ste 202-412, St. Augustine, Florida, 32092,
USA

Printed in Great Britain
by Amazon

80326604R00066